H*desde*ong Kong

Poets in conversation with Octavio Paz

on the occasion of the poet's centenary

Para Anabel y Robert, amigos y cómplices de aventuras. ¡Los quiero!

Collegeville PA. 14/3/21

A Chameleon Press book

DESDE HONG KONG
ISBN 978-988-18623-0-3

© 2014 individual contributors & Chameleon Press Ltd.

Published by Chameleon Press Ltd.
15/F, 1506-7 Pacific Plaza, 418 Des Voeux Road West, Hong Kong
www.chameleonpress.com

First printing 2014

Chameleon Press and the poets wish to acknowledge previous publication of:

"Fantastic Ganglion" (Gémino H. Abad) in *Nameable Days: Poems Revisited*, University of the Philippines Press, 2014

"A River on Its Way" (Tammy Ho Lai-Ming) in *Not A Muse*, Haven Books, 2010

"Release from Darkness" and "Rajasthan in the Rains" (Racha Joshi) in *Crossing the Vaitarani: Journeys*, Writer's Workshop, Kolkata 2008

"Vanilla in the Stars" (Agnes S. L. Lam) in *Nosside 2008: XXIVth Poetry Prize anthology*, Centro Studi Bosio

"Words Lost" (Aaron Maniam) in *Morning at Memory's Border*, Firstfruits Publications, 2005

"Writing History" (David McKirdy) in *Ancestral Worship*, Chameleon Press, 2014 and *Asian Cha*, 2002

"Water" and "Rain" (Danton Remoto) in *Skin Voices Faces: Poems*, Anvil Publishing, 1991

"North" (Madeleine Slavick) in *Prairie Schooner, vol. 6*, 2013; "The Act of Walking" in *delicate access*, 2004 and *Writing Macao*, 2003

"Emerald City Blues" (Phoebe Tsang) in *Contents of a Mermaid's Purse*, Tightrope Books, 2009

"The Last Days of Octavio Paz" (translation of Wang Jixian by Diana Shi & George O'Connell) in *2008 Atlanta Review China Edition* and the *Spring 2013 Pangolin House*

Hong *desde* Kong

Poets in conversation
with Octavio Paz
on the occasion of the
poet's centenary

chameleon press
hong kong

Introduction

OCTAVIO PAZ is a living poet. His towering presence in the world of literature is still felt today, for he unveils the beauty in words that lay bare the inner workings of human nature.

Paz the poet is also an alchemist who synthesises lyricism and sophisticated intellect yet whose words nevertheless remain grounded in everyday life. He may be timeless but his earthly existence could not have had any better backdrop than the troubled twentieth century and, in particular, Mexico, a country riddled with conflicts and contradictions. Those difficult times were, paradoxically, a vital source of energy for his creative process.

Paz was unique. By intellect and instinct, he distrusted utopias of any kind, exposing them, whether political or aesthetic. Always passionate, he might be called "The Last Surrealist"; Surrealism was a reference throughout his whole life:

> A tree's grown inwards
> from my temples.
> Veins are its roots
> nerves its branches
> and thoughts its tangle of leaves.
> —from "A tree within" (Árbol adentro)

A convinced liberal and democrat, his creativity was forged by his conscience, which became a crucible for his social and aesthetic criticism. He used to say that by living the present, we enjoy our share of eternity. Chronos sets us a trap. Paz unlocks the shackles of the past while untying the knot of an anguished future.

Octavio Paz's poetry is a tribute to life. *The Double Flame*[1] of our existence crackles between the deep blue and the red in all his

---

[1] The title of one of his most representative works.

works. The flame is all life, intensity and heat: eroticism and love, consciousness and integrity.

From very early on, Paz was enticed by the cultures and literary traditions of India, China and Japan, echoes of which permeate his work. In his travels in the East and in his studies, he discovered a new way of seeing poetry and life. In his reach and depth, he continues to be the inspiration for new creative work.

Octavio Paz would have turned one hundred on 31 March this year; we thought that the best way to remember this great poet would be to spark a creative process and invite poets to contribute their own work inspired by him. The result of the overwhelming response is this poetic "conversation" that crosses decades, cultures and oceans.

The link between Paz and Hong Kong—a city both Chinese and cosmopolitan, that beats with an incredibly vital rhythm—is a natural one. This collection of poems by fellow poets from Hong Kong, Asia and beyond is a worthy tribute to a man who knew no borders.

German Muñoz, Tammy Ho Lai-Ming, Juan José Morales
Hong Kong, August 2014

Contents

A la memoria de Octavio Paz

poems

I Talk to Myself — I Talk to You[1]

by Mani Rao

Paz: Man is inhabited by silence and space
How to sate his hunger,
How to populate his space?
How to escape my own image?[2]

Sade via Madame de Saint-Ange:
By repeating our attitudes and postures in a
thousand different ways, they infinitely multiply
those same pleasures for the persons seated here
upon this ottoman. Thus everything is visible, no
part of the body can remain hidden: everything must
be seen; these images are so many groups disposed
around those enchained by love, so many delicious
tableaux[3]

Celan: I hear that they call life
our only refuge[4]

Faiz: Never mind if there'll be no wine in hell -
At least the preacher will be nowhere around

Chitre: Will I ever find heaven's fucking light?[5]

Paz: Perhaps, behind that door
There is no other side[6]

Symborska: So he's got to have happiness,
he's got to have truth, too,
he's got to have eternity -
did you ever![7]

2

Paz: Nirvana is Samsara,
  Samsara is not Nirvana[8]

P.K.: if one day
  you find
  a more spacious
  more tolerant
  happy land

  a more civilized
  peaceful and resilient garden
  I'll be glad to watch you go.[9]

Octavio Paz had a lifelong interest in the Marquis de Sade's writings. Paz writes in 1964 that he read Sade "with astonishment and horror, with curiosity and disgust, with admiration and recognition." In 1960, he writes about Sade as a discomfiting interlocutor. In 1986, he calls him a kind-hearted man. For Paz, "Sade did not vanish." I imagine that such a sustained engagement is more than response, it is a dialog, for Sade's writing *spoke* to Paz. Poem enters a timeless space, and all speakers past, present and future are in conversation with each other, Paz speaks to us, and we speak to him and hear others speaking to him. And PK Leung who no longer meets you and me for dinner in Hong Kong joins us in the response.

[1] Paz, Octavio. "Letter of Testimony." Translated by Eliot Weinberger. *The Collected Poems 1957-1987*. London: Paladin Poetry, 1991. p. 621.
[2] Paz. "The Prisoner." Translated by Eliot Weinberger. *An Erotic Beyond: Sade*. New York and London: Harcourt Brace & Company, 1998. p. 5.
[3] Sade, The Marquis de. Translated by Richard Seaver and Austryn Wainhouse. *Justine, Philosophy in the Bedroom, & Other Writings*. New York: Grove Press, 1990. p. 203.
[4] Celan, Paul. "Schneepart." Translated by Michael Hamburger. *Selected Poems*. London and New York: Penguin, 1996. p. 331.
[5] Faiz, Ahmed Faiz. "Quatrain." Translated by Shiv K. Kumar. *Selected Poems*. New Delhi: Viking, 1995. p. 91.
[6] Chitre, Dilip. "Will I ever find." *As Is, Where Is*. Mumbai: Poetrywallah, 2014. p. 236.
[7] Symborska, Wislawa. "No End of Fun." Translated by Stanislaw Baranczak and Clare Cavanagh. *View with a Grain of Sand – Selected Poems*. Great Britain: Faber & Faber, 1996. p. 60.
[8] Paz, Octavio. "Reading John Cage." Translated by Eliot Weinberger. *The Collected Poems*. p. 237.
[9] Leung, PK. "At the Grave of Mr. Cai Jiemin." Translated by Yau Wai Ping. *Travelling with a Bitter Melon*. Hong Kong: Asia 2000, 2000. p. 337.

A Tree Ordained

by Kit Fan

> *A tree's grown inwards*
> *from my temples.*
> — *"Árbol adentro" - "A tree within"*

Smoked herring-leaves hanging
on fallen branches on maggot-white
ember-soil. Five barefoot monks
walking on wood-corpses. Ash-snow
falling in Cardamom Forest and there is
nothing inward about devastation.

In Areng valley wild grasses half as tall
as elephants glistened like emeralds
after downpours and down the steep
elephant corridor Siamese crocodiles
bathed in grassy rivers where the scales
of wild fish shimmered in the eddies.

Saffron-robed, the last unfellable one
stands ordained like a cenotaph
for the aurochs, quagga, dodo.
Wind-voices from the burnt, to-be-
submerged villages saying *let's*
leave our tree and sell our buffalo.

Between Hoping and Losing
by Jennifer Wong

the sun is altering us:
the day is one among many
supposed we were to carry on like this
which is perhaps unsatisfactory.
Between the hope
and losing you, is it your touch
or your lightest promise
that has convinced me?
To hope is a good cause to believe.
The day after you told me the story.
Habits I find difficult to leave.
How about the growing space
between us, what shall we
fill it with? The layer of sand
reverberates with heat. What if
intimacy belongs to someone else.
When you look at me
as you do so now
is that sadness or love?
When the tide comes,
the landscape will feel different.
Our sky changes by the minute.
Between losing and hoping
we have our choices,
but the sun has blinded us.

Close Your Eyes, See As a Ghost Sees
by Kit Kelen

> *to see, to touch each day's lovely forms*
> *—"Hymn among the ruins"*

1.
two stars fell
this made a sky
there had to be a watching world
moon to pale

every sky
will yet lie fallen
and within a tree's reach

so the storm is dreaming
in the cloud

the sky is there because trees touch

the tree and its fellows bask, drink in
they are drawing clouds over

the tree is a tribe of welcoming passages

when no one's looking
so leaves speak

the wind
locks itself
in the stone
in the tree

one word
not silence
snow said
till it melts

the tree is all creatures
reluctant to learn their own names

in a word
so many of us meet
and the trace we leave
while imperceptible
remains to the word's eternity
however brief that may be

2.
blue of the sky is one
but the night is many in stars
just one of these can be the truth
and the truth is what's not telling

how few the moments
the heart's steps are heard
the breath of night is rarely noted
even the smell of ripening wheat
is something the farmer turns indoors from

and the choking fumes
of the waste laden river
how little time we give these

just one way
past the delusions of grandeur
to give full rein
ride hard till you fall

as a ghost sees, longs to touch
so close your eyes

and they come
the two worlds of color
one under your eyelids
one deeper in

there isn't a bridge between
you must set sail in the bath of toys
so many days the far shore
in a nautical sort of house like a light
grey harbor of nightfall
brought to berth

draw your own map
find world to fit

only to closed eyes
will the colors come
all your own making

none of it ever meant as such
it's only a shadow
this touch
the line cast

there's a pocket full of strange coins I remember
and though it was only the sea that was singing
I could read every word

Two Birds, One Tree

by Koon Woon

Two birds, one tree
Two birds in one tree argue
over its span, its symbolic reach,
the meaning of it all, the seeds,
the fallen leaves,
finalized by gravity.

Two men in one boat discuss
the ripples on water,
the bob and the line,
the murky depths,
in fathoms beneath.

Four creatures thus converse
across the elements of
wind and water,
growth and grossness
of life and its demise.

That the wind may blow
and water perturbates,
that men and birds imitate
the world's inadvertent sounds,
as time is lost and we lose ground
the note and the nodes,
its liveliness casually found.

Subsolar/Sublunar

by Louise Ho

From among great stone temples
Engraved tablets
Primed to planetary rhythms
Chronometer of the spheres
Articulating the land and its people
Interpreting earth's habits
Singing the elements to wake or to sleep
Come to us
Your sun drenched golden sussuras.

At this end of the earth
Moon-lit
Floating island
Glides among shadows
With ballast of granite and concrete.
It has
Weathered many a storm,
And the biggest of them
May yet turn it upside down.

Then, will it heave and hitch
Into position of magnetic repel,
Thence to bounce itself off
To right itself in the end,
This, our tiny jagged moon-rock?

Word Un-worded
by Louise Ho

Converge on the dissolute
Then centrifugally destroy
Whatever is made unmade
Known unknowable
Unknown
Saying it unsayable
Unsaid
Found now
Lost now.

In subterranean caverns -
Septic miasma.
Flee quickly, the canary has slumped.
Language is lethal,
Words their agents.
Images on the edge
Of the liminal,
They too can kill.

Swallow your words,
Choke on them
If need be.
There is neither time nor space
For speech of any kind.
Squeeze between a rock and a hard place,
Between Paz's "shutting up"
And Beckett's "Breath".

Winter Clocks

by Kate Rogers

after "Between going and staying"

Keep slow time like metronomes set larghetto.
Each tick is audible, and followed by a conscious
pause.
Time is sluggish: a frog hibernating
in the icy mud coating the lake bottom.

Even the digital minutes shift shape - 7 to 8 -
with tremulous slowness. Clock hands
are blunt knives, only good for cutting
soft cheese. Time is sliced thick
piled on the curbs, in cold white slabs.

In Toronto, at the bus stop,
huddled coats, hoods up.
Only breath is visible - its cartoon speech balloon
emptied of questions. At barely five pm,
darkness streams from the tap.
I go to bed early.

In opposite time, outside my empty Hong Kong flat,
Sai Ying Pun market crashes awake at dawn.
Metal awnings spring back,
people descend from surrounding Tong Lau's.
The best cut of pork arrives still bleeding.
At the corner fruit stall shoppers palpate oranges.
The sun rises full of juice.

Writing History

by David McKirdy

Chinese gentlemen in traditional robes
inhabit the streets of my youth
scribes with folding tables and chairs
inkstone and brushes
gaunt classical scholars
performing exquisite calligraphy - for utility
in the service of
illiterate laborers.
The highest expression of the literary arts
reduced to mere communication.

Letters home to be read and narrated
by others, in other streets in other cities.
Part fortune-teller, psychologist, agony-uncle
bad news censored, rendered palatable
with subtlety and nuance
good tidings enhanced.

In another place, another time
they would be
magistrates, court officials
rather than abroad in significance
at the sharp end of the historical narrative
the collective amanuensis of a country in chaos.

The Word is a Country

by Eddie Tay

after "The word outloud"

The word is a country
that refuses to speak,

has passports
that tell you where to go.

I have served my time
with my rifle and combat boots.

I've cut my way through thickets
and still the country escapes me.

Quietly, it tells me to go elsewhere,
so my wife cannot hear.

Quietly, it tells me to dream of periwinkles
though I have no love for mollusks.

The word is a stone shell
I beat my head with.

Until, caught in its labyrinth,
I am unable to speak

I walk so no one would see
the spiral scar at the back of my head.

The word is a spinning galaxy,
a godly sun I hide from.

I dare not say
periwinkle, periwinkle, periwinkle.

Water

by Danton Remoto

For you, my lover, I will be like water.
I will be Loch Lomond flowing
In loneliness from Ardlui to Arden.

I will be the Falls of Dochart hurling itself
Down the hills of Breadalbane,
The rocks rumbling with my cascading force.

I will be the rain, slanting
Over Stirling in needles tiny as pores.
I will be the snowflakes, drifting

From the Orkney to the Isle of Skye,
Falling in silent fury, as if focusing themselves
In the cold eye of memory.

For you, my lover, I will be like water.

Rain

by Danton Remoto

This morning, it is raining
In my country.
Water slides down
The leaves,
Like tongue on skin.

The sound of their falling
Collects
Like breath on the lobes
Of ears.

You are a continent away.
There, the leaves are beginning
To turn.
Soon, night will steal hours
From day,
And snow will be whirling
In drifts.

But you are here,
In the country
Of my mind,
Wiping away the maps
Of mist
On the window pane,
Lying in bed beside me,
As the pulse of the pillows and sheets -
Even the very breath of rain -
Begins to quicken.

Footsteps on the Viaduct
by Wong Pui Ying

1. Here or there

The place does not exist, existed.
Absence that is also presence.
Silence is born of sound,
sound, silence.
Love is the river in which you drown your gazes.
Pain is the tree that sprouts out of your body.

2. The meaning of lotus

Are you the purity that enshrines the flower?
Are you the brotherhood that entangles its root?

I'm purity like water purged of its crime.
I'm brotherhood like tendrils ripped by currents.

3. Continent of one

In the train I'm almost asleep.
Valley or meadow, graffiti or barb wire,
night drives through me
like time's little coffin.

4. The track

Let dark complete the coupling
Click by click let the light fall.

After the Sunstone

by Michellan Alagao

Your forever arriving
is my never-ending goodbye:
y llega siempre, walang hanggang paalam;
both with things lost in translation.
When you talk about things
appearing without urgency
I do not fully understand,
because the waters that pour out prophesies,
I drink.
The journey to days of future present past,
I take.
That misery which shines like a bird,
I sing to. It sings back.
The goddess whose body you traverse,
she is my mother - nourished me with water and blood.
All her likenesses are me/not me.
All her forms and configurations are me/not me.
The sharpness. The star-brightness.
Poet, abre los ojos.
Speak clearly to me.
Know my urgency.
Efimera outside the window;
the roadside weeds we passed the day before.
Our bodies are ill and fading.
Let the double-edged light
pierce through the division,
shadow from spirit.
The snake sheds its skin;
the chrysalis in full, bursts.
We are forever departing
and eternally arriving.

Vanilla in the Stars

by Agnes Lam

When I was a child,
I used to gaze at the stars above

our garden of roses, jasmine and *lingzhi* by the sea,
wondering how far away they really were,
whether they were shining still at the source
by the time their light reached me ...

I was told that everyone was born with a star
which glowed or dimmed with the fortunes of each.
I also heard people destined to be close
were at first fragments of the same star

and from birth went searching for each other.
Such parting, seeking, reuniting might take
three lifetimes with centuries in between.
I had thought all these were but myths ...

Now decades later, I read about the life of stars,
how their cores burn for ten billion years,
how towards the end, just before oblivion,
they atomize into nebulae of fragile brilliance -

ultra violet, infra red, luminous white, neon green or blue,
astronomical butterflies of gaseous light
afloat in a last waltz choreographed by relativity,
scattering their heated ashes into the void of the universe ...

Some of this cosmic dust falls onto our little earth
carrying hydrocarbon compounds, organic matter
able to mutate into plant and animal life,
a spectrum of elemental fragrances ...

Perhaps on the dust emanating from one ancient star
were borne the first molecules of a *pandan* leaf,
a sprig of mint or basil, a vanilla pod, a vine tomato,
a morning frangipani, an evening rose, a lily of the night ...

Perhaps our parents or grandparents or ancestors further back
strolling through a garden or a field had breathed in the scents
effusing from some of these plants born of the same star
and passed them on as DNA in the genes of which we were made ...

Could that be why, on our early encounters, we already sensed
in each other a whiff of something familiar, why, when we are near,
there is in the air some spark which seems to have always been
        there,
prompting us to connect our pasts, share our stories even as they
        evolve ...

... till the day when we too burn away into dust
and the aromas of our essence dissipate
into the same kaleidoscope of ether light
to be drawn into solar space by astral winds ...

... perhaps to make vanilla in a star to be
before the next lifetime of three?

Ji Dan Hua

by George O'Connell

> *When I am undone,*
> *When I am no one.*
> — Roethke

Their scent descends
in nearly jasmine notes,
the white blooms still unbruised,
the sunny yolk,
as though waiting in each throat
were the nectar
for some slender tongue.

From you I learned the Mandarin
ji dan hua
long before its English
frangipani, plumeria.

They fall across the concrete path,
loosed by wind or rain or season.
Now and then
I slip three stems between my skull
and its red bandana,
breathing what I'll scatter on your desk.

How selfish my old heart
someday to stain
yours for their fragrance.

Soap

by George O'Connell

Milk of goats, milk of olives,
oil of lily or of palm,
pumice of burnt stone.
From the touch of your mother
to the last unnameable hands
so many times
more than any lover
the pale cake's tallow and lye
slide along your ribs,
soils dissolving, years
rinsed clear.

How thin the white tether,
each morning's kiss of lather,
goodnight to all your days,
the mirrored face of your father
your hand's own blade.

Beginning

by Page Richards

He said a god was there.
I followed right away

left my black shoes
in the hallway, the ones my mother tried

to toss out weeks before,
I left them tucked under

red boots and snow-filled slippers,
I lined them all backwards

right on left, left on right.
So before I left down the stairs

gliding down the handrail
covering the metal with light sweat

of excitement I covered the mat
with a glaze of powder to keep them

when the red car came humming
against the curb and my bag ready

without strappy shoes, the heaviest
trip I would take, leaving them all behind.

Pilgrimage

by Page Richards

A mysterious voice heard me
in the middle of my years, took me to water

which ran back down so I could follow,
what do you want? it asked

and I, the youngest of my family
without shoes I never liked to give up

wanted to get on my knees in water
peel off my life, bring them all back

bring back my father, my mother back
to me, all. I counted on them I said

while a false lion not far off
sat on the hill and looked left

for no reason other than scent
or sound or something

he could tell in his body.
I crawled up to the mysterious voice

and asked to be let in, let into what?
the silly voice asked, into something

I said. You talk the whole time he said,
I know I said, as if my voice could do something.

Octaves for O. Paz

by José Ángel Araguz

la luz descalza sobre el mar y la tierra dormidos[1]

O, let's go walking then, like
the light across the ocean,
and the light across the land.
no one will hear us. pages
in a book rest with a light,
you saw it once. I am here
to tell you it remains: light,
O, dances: barefoot, soundless.

de la piedra/abierta por la mirada[2]

that is the feeling that came:
the story of your visit
to the famous poet who
made you wait: you saw him mark
out words, scribble more, again
mark: you asked why: he said to
make the automatic more
automatic: O, I see -

mis palabras se volvieron visibles un instante[3]

Joseph Cornell has us beat:
we look in fascinated,
faces made water for a
moment, water that reflects
meaning, not thought but a light
past thought, glimmer, and glint of
what is found: O, what did you
find: O, the box shuts us out.

sobre la hoja de papel
el poema se hace
como el día
sobre la palma del espacio[4]

could we write: *morning, window,*
light: and write: *afternoon stretched,*
and so on: write past things missed
by the eye, missed by being
alive, write: *the tree outside:*
the feeling of lines moving
past you, write: *the paper wind*
moves: O, we'd miss the missing.

    La realidad es más real en blanco y negro[5]

paper, again: poet, ink.
what you would say on paper
to paper: what you would say,
ink, again. poet: pebbles
of breath, until the breath is
paper: still paper, again,
in the hands. poet, you ink
too fast: paper, still your hands.

---

[1] These syllabic octaves riff off of end lines from poems by Octavio Paz. This first comes
    from "Domingo en la isla de Elefanta".
[2] "Piedra Blanca y Negra"
[3] "Objectos y Apariciones"
[4] "El Fuego de Cada Día"
[5] "Cara al Tiempo"

la alegría
de los vivos
es la pena de los muertos[6]

pity, my reality:
to dance while dust dithers, drums
softly. is that you rising
as I thumb your *Collected*,
pace the room to stay awake -
important, the dust, the dance
from black, white, and back again.
is that you: paper laughing -

el cielo anda en la tierra[7]

heart of the water: you write,
your hand, like mine, earthbrown, kept
on wrestling with daybreak,
that time itself a battle:
color over color break
the sky over the earth of
my hand, O, where the sky you
saw keeps walking in each heart.

estoy
en el espacio
etcétera[8]

O, the vine, the kind that turns
itself through, around fences:
were you to try to follow,
leaf to leaf, the light would rise,
turn in its own way, you would
forget where you started, which
leaf, this leaf, perhaps, and on,
turning through, around your words.

desmemoria me guía
hacia el reverso de la vida[9]

O, what will be forgotten
last: words, stray hair on the neck,
where the water glass was placed,
the pitcher's weight in your hand
before, after, the water's
push on glass, clear as nothing,
push on itself, nothing clear
except the now: which now last -

[6] "Epitafio de una vieja"
[7] "Madrugada al raso"
[8] "Reversible"
[9] "A Través"

The Distance Between Rain and You

by Timothy Kaiser

I tuck you in against the cold,
Your silver breath
Rising against the rain.
"Let's find a real place",
You muffle,
"A place where history
Sulks back into walls.
Where bliss
Hangs on the precipice
Of a solitary word".

Your voice again,
Polished by waves,
I hear now through my half empty bottle,
Through a half lit bar,
As your nails climb my thigh.
Hear you as the day
Fades into late o'clock murmurs.
Hear you as I hear the rain
Inviting me
To risk joy,
To abandon time for the wantonness of words,
To fashion fire from shadows,
Shadows from mist,
Mist from dew.

Just past midnight
We hear the rain pause,
And tip together out the door.
With one hand stroking yours
The other strangling my bottle,
We splash and whoop into moons
Rippling our sidewalk.
"Do you trust the ferment of spring?"
You ask before my lips
Find yours in an alleyway.
The sound of rain
Encasing us
In its gathering swell.

North

by Madeleine Slavick

milky air
silent plains

it could be snow
this might be another country

crossing the Yangtze
we are grace in the making

and the train hums
like a man I want to love

bare trees appear
singular in winter bodies

oversized nests
must be minds

I hear wind and morning
locked in a room

count nine plastic bags
under four clouds

mud, cigarettes
cold hands

cities grow rings
nests remain

this country and I live
hardly speaking with each other
and snow has landed

The Act of Walking

by Madeleine Slavick

we ask
is walking and freedom the same thing?
the way we step
into stride
with the soft scissors of our metronome arms
sometimes we hum

how the head searches forward:
around the corner could be god
or a barricade of opinion
what does the sidewalk protect?

one, two horns sounding
tick goes the ear   small goes the eye
nothing lives the same as yesterday
we do not need a purpose
to know this moment

please,
a slow seeing is the revolution of kindness

A River On Its Way

by Tammy Ho Lai-Ming

I give, and I give, and I give. It's the way it is.
Like a river feeding itself to the ocean.
The pattern's not undone, yet.
There may be rocks, obstructing the way.
Or lesser streams forking from my body,
And drying up in the sun.
A traveller may pause, squat next to my belly
Where an accidental leaf rattles like a canoe,
Cup a mouthful of what makes me me.
Still, the pattern's not undone.
Like a river feeing itself to the ocean -
Child, I continue to give myself to you
Until I become undone - scattered pockets
Of primitive earth, pealed bare.

In Salzburg

by Isabela Banzon

where everything seems a long way
from the Philippines, where six hours
behind, in April, it rained all day, the landscape
like faces, white as snow on the Alps,
the architecture boldly baroque not tropical
(certainly sunshine and rain and ventilation
always on my mind), Mozart for real
not digital nor on vinyl, the banana smoothie
and cakes at the university Town Center
not quite the finest coffee and strudel combination
at the stumbled upon Carpe Diem's (though
of course so European Union in price);

jetlagged, in a jumper and matching overcoat,
braving the spring weather, the unimaginable
eight degrees celsius, you just a tourist
feeling your way around town, so unlike
you and the summer you just left
where the kapok have burst and float
like a bombardment of thoughts in seeming
abandon in air, then settle on grass, and wind
from the desk fan you bequeathed mimics
gusts from the gentle northeasterlies...
So in reply to your letter (I'm using your
portable wifi), it's still warm as bread popping up
from your toaster, the eggs still unpoached,
your muesli in the fridge still untouched.
When I go out to replenish the rest
of the pantry, I walk the stretch we always take,
where at the pedestrian lane cars don't stop
for us still, as if in the world no one cares truly.

The Brilliance of This

by Les Wicks

after "Sun stone" & "Between going and staying"

You don't dissolve in water.
Water waits for stone
it's the throne, bone, the judge's gravel.
Your fingers are life, we must be dying.

We have all these walls
mountains in light.
We pay for them, then paint
every 3 years.
We wait for rivers & desire, constant companions.

You said
I'm fantastic that leaves me
in a state of chance. Why me?
The louring lake. You when you're best.
Me too.
Guitar scar. Paragon.
It can't work
but nothing does.

You worry too much.
        I worry too little. We are
        a match.

Do Not Speak to Me Like Rain
by Reid Mitchell

You speak to me in sounds of rain, in consonants
plosive, in vowels blown by wind, topped into mud
Every word must decide for herself, himself
whether to die at birth

You pretend this pitter patter is diffidence
that it gives me a chance to instead breathe
the ozoned-air, roots pushing, seeds
germinating

You pretend this raining night clouding
the mood will not succumb
to the harsh sun that withers our words
into one stark meaning

You pretend lovers are passionate
kind, forbearing mannikins arrayed
with this season's hat and next season's
gloves

You pretend that when the rains wash out
gullies and the gullies rot into gulches
no yellow dog will find the sparrow bones
my deaf heart left behind

Golden Gate

by Tim Suermondt

Each rooftop is peeling lightly
yet still dazzling
in the afternoon Easter air,
like the New Damascus
I dreamed of last night.

A woman across the courtyard
opens her window, waving
a cherry purple scarf
for good luck in any kind of love.

My wife marks the sights
she's dying to see, cheerfully
determined to dragging me
through as much of the city
as is humanly possible.

I start struggling to uncork
a bottle of wine and find
my socks, missing the blue yacht
going by big in the distance.
My wife says it was magnificent.

Firsthand Account of Myself

by James Shea

Empty street, no wind.
Just a hanging cord
of the window curtain
after I unleashed it.
I'm living a cappella.
A floor paved with air.
A house glittering with rain.
A single forgiveness
built into the sin.

Phreas
by Dino Mahoney

released
the pebble falls,

bristling ear
feels

the shadow of a whisper
of a splash,

something sleeping,
woken,

something not there,
there,

something stirring
under the table,

mother,
mineral,

a liquid
gulp,

an unword
answering

a swallowed
question.

Ginger Flower Fields

by Elbert Siu Ping Lee

Crows descend in formation
on telephone lines
that drape across the evening sky.

In ginger flower fields
they dug and they found
pig bones, chicken bones, and human bones.

Ginger flowers writhe in the simmering heat.
In the dark, they glow.

Strewn across a shady patch were remains
of smothered uniforms,
of party lines and news lines from heaven, clan and bloodlines
      from below.

Wild, wild, ginger flowers,
they spread-fast,
after the summer rain.

On the bones they found no tattoo.
Some bones managed to miss the graveyard -
the last stand
of human boundaries.

The scent of ginger flowers is unmistakable,
especially in a hot musty night.
It bodes well with the markings on the cemented tombs.
These evoke memories.

Waiting for the advent of a new line
to tag along that meandering path that leads to nowhere,
the crows ascend slowly
into the night sky.

Words Lost

by Aaron Maniam

> *"Between what I dream and what I forget - poetry."*
> — *Octavio Paz*

What happens to the words we lose?
Shadow-light, feather-friendly, elusive
As dreams that flutter away,
Borne by a wakening eyelid's breeze?

Words from moments
When rhymes and cadences find their places
Before the crowning of an exquisite full stop
When quotidian questions meld with the metaphysical
When a friend, long-dead, returns in a reverie
And we manage to chat about life
And love and striving to be happy ...

You know the words I mean:
Those we manage to hold fast to
While floating through the amniotic drowse
Of semi-sleep or almost-awake ...
Their familiar fellow-feel nourished
By something more ancient than friendship
Or even family. They teach us
What it means to know something
So profoundly that we hear it
Live - yet so little that
Once a wakeful start snips
At the frail umbilical string
Connecting us, it floats away
While we, with all we have,
To retreating shadows cling ...

Soon I will wake,
Wonder where they go,
Those words we lose
On our way to wakefulness ...
And from this middle-state,
This between-world straddling
Memory and Dream, will come the ache
Of words that recede from recollection
Before they start to be, or even seem.

If We Are a Metaphor of the Universe

by Nicholas YB Wong

If on the verge I lure capitalism to sleep over
If selfhood is redeemable from shelves of condoms at 7-11
If I confuse packaged emotions with intentions
If this is why I was water drop in my fourth grade school play
If wishing emotions expired like anecdotes
If reality is best read with a fictional mindset and you know it
If on second thought capitalism rejects me to have more time
    and space
If on second thought I thought he was full of that time and space
If not catching the calm and the asking of his breath
If he recommends sleeping instead with politics
If politics is likely, as he says, more anatomical, showy and loud
If scandals only work with fame and I am not worried
If mixing the certification of the self with social science is not a
    fault
If a fault can be undone like I am undone
If we anagram capitalism to *I am plastic*
If the madness and madeness of recycling is self-contained
If it is more expensive to burn feelings than to buy them
If most things that can be bought are bought out of stillness
If things include stocks, children, companionship
If stillness costs
If lies are sponsored vernacular of truths
If they are they are they are are they and you know it
If a pulse in pusillanimity breaks from a continuum of beats
If lumpy initials of corporates laugh on swings invisibly
If it is natural to hear iron chains screech because the wind blows
If please remove me from the list
If listing lust on the walls of a tormented love shaft
If you see my love is a red, red hose
If setting foot on half a sky

If a frog in a well knows it has swum in creeks as a tadpole,
      unashamed
If the well suddenly wants to travel but what to take with its
      hollow torso
If a pulse is willing to pay a rainforest of commissions to have its
      own thoughts
If torsos are towed to a compulsory stop
If flesh is a commitment to melancholy and the lack of interest in
      connecting
If dice can do nothing, if days can do nothing
If citizenship is a menu of 15 courses
If it also makes this nice zip around your lips

Between Going and Coming
by Collier Nogues

Whether one wants
or doesn't want to go outside,

outside is always color
in particular, and grain.

A saw whirs on a balcony,
the street sweeper accelerates,

a woman shows her sister to the door.
The ear gathers evidence

for the mind to rhyme in memory,
the thousand parts

which surface in their glitter: the hospital
where I was born no longer stands,

cast iron rusts in a foreign flood,
how dearly bought a friend's marriage was.

The neighbor couple comes home
and lets themselves in. Inside

the foghorn, all freqencies, all raining
together condensed

on the sides of the metal,
I reach for the total,

for the words "all" and "every".
Another neighbor holds his screen door open.

He hammers. He quiets
the birds by whistling.

He quits.
The comfort that someone may choose

to pause,
may pause long enough to recede

like a tide who knows it won't come back in,
who knows she's ending, as my mother did -

the shifts back and forth
should be thicker than a whistle

but even these same chairs, with their wet feet,
were here the last time she was.

The day splits open perfectly evenly.
The halves are fresh from the sea.

The Wake

by Collier Nogues

The white wake lasts.
The shape it makes,
the water's bother,
lasts longer.

The boat's first cut
spines like a feather
then feathers out around
a gown

whose hem shrinks
from the ghost within it.
That first cut is a limit.
Morning locusts

heat the air with their
grated sudden silence.
Stranger
than the figure

is its ground, white
and slack, the motor
cut and quiet.
Wakeless

the boat lolls in the water.
Tilts, someone leans off it.
Begins a slow summer,
clouded over

whose wet splashes
in between become
dropped cans of what
the men are drinking.

If two watch together
they warn each other
of the wake they can
see coming.

And then there's wind,
which means a storm.
The boat comes home,
its work done.

It comes home having
woken the whole shore,
having worked the water
out of its system.

The waves will reel
a long time before
they're free of our
instructions.

The Translated Word

by Douglas Robinson

The word telekinetic,
floating up off the translated page,
echoing glossolalic
through HKG's international gates,
400 souls knuckled white
into the paging of delayed flight
CX 850 to Mexico City,
topping the tarmac to walk
that tightwire tensed
from the silenced cry
to the corporate cool
of the inflight magazine

in three languages.

"To speak a foreign tongue,
and understand it,
and translate it into one's own
     is to restore
     the unity
        of the beginning,"
wrote Octavio Paz,
that beginning *blanco como el ánima*
that rises off the page like echolalia,
that compulsion to translate
that inclined Paz to think
     "that we are once more
     in the presence
     of a human constant."

Bare beginning, תִּישׁאַרְב, *bereshit*
bara Elohim et hashamayim
ve'et ha'arets, when the earth was
without form and empty, that gorm-
lessness of the unity that
    as Paz hoped
translation has already restored,
    the bareness before the Elohim
(those impetuous Palestinian gods)
went and created one language
but then scattered our speech (תֵפָּ, *saphah*),
dispersed (זְפָּו, *wayyapes*) us like tourists to 1000 airports,
lest we build an Airbus big enough
and with the metaphysical fuel capacity
to fly us all to the gates of heaven
      and so become
like the Elohim themselves.

Innocence in no sense
      other than
wanting the words
to miss our flight.

Fantastic Ganglion

by Gémino H. Abad

I

How subtly this fantastic ganglion makes division!
It will first heighten the distinctness of matter
And from such deadly soil, quicken into mind -
A leap that makes comic the ponderous centuries
Left desolate with gills, a foot, and a mantle.

Messengers of this oracle often expire
Before their words are audible,
But hunger, diligence, and a humble fury
Shall yield the soul her eyes to make her whole
And, like the wild flower, a phenomenon of splendor.

Where the world hides its horrors and scandals,
A fateful glimpse unveils the larger truth
And makes of the instant a deliverer of time,
A way of being, a knowledge of things beyond their words,
All lesser glories, unremembered loss.

The soul then, purged of smaller illuminations,
Yields her tenure of truth so light may redeem,
Even as the stars dissolve, for intimation of sun,
And the enormous silence of the sky
Gathers their ruins in the sudden flood.

So great a part of her secretive being
Is the way to the soul, afflicted with dark.
She dismisses empires with such perfect indifference
The flickering mind acquires a habit of reluctance
To spread her spirit abroad in daylight's hum and drum.

II

Death sulks with his mean possibilities,
The horrors of his envy too limited.
The sockets of the eye fill merely with dirt,
The skull only trophy of his broken realm;
And the worm, no respecter of sanctity,

Come to analyze the dregs of thought,
The shells of worded mysteries,
Too final, too prosaic for belief -
What if it were death's squiggly angel,
Its rampant calligraphy is all but ash.

O, yet the body never had beliefs,
Neither in life nor hereafter.
As the sounds of humanity grow dim,
A tolling as from a distant, inhospitable star,
Not death, nor life, can insist on debts.

This body had only once a greed
As exhalation from the center of things
That the mind wooed for their truth;
How but for such deep and gentle wooing
Did things at last acquire a voice, a musical power?

And so the body did soon require alien food,
An appetite that grew like an essential torment,
And thereby it knew at last it was its own soul,
And death having come, its soul now lays
Its flesh to rest, as the wind too helps the leaf to earth.

Dead Wood

by Michael O'Sullivan

A myna bird instinctively moves to alight in
the space where a tree's branch once stretched
like an amputee reaching down
to scratch a limb forever severed.

A forlorn dumpster truck driver in jeans and polo-shirt
Leans forward in his passenger seat
Looking for all the world like a broken man
As his boss, the chainsaw wielder, replaces his chain.

The fifty foot ficus tree was too much for the
two-foot long single blade of the blue chainsaw.
Now the driver is up again, perched like a teenager
On the edge of the back seat, controlling the digger's arm,
texting at breaks.

Virtouso-like, he manouevres the metal joysticks
As the digger's mouth collects gangly boughs and trunks like
a beak collecting dead worms or tindersticks,
Intricate life-infested arms once open to sky and sea and the
      angry swells
Of typhoons crack and whine as dogs sniff their still warm
      entrails.

"There'll be more room for parking now" I shout in despair
"It's only space for one car really" replies the London-educated
Son of the non-English speaking village mayor, rocking on his
        heels,
"We have papers from the Land department"
"Did they say knock both trees, the living and the dead? I can't
        read them, they're in Chinese"
"I can't read them either" he replies.
The documents in plastic pockets holding brownish puddles lie
        scattered across the gravel.

Myna birds still scuttle through corridors of flight
Defamiliarized now by the lack of nesting, forraging, hang-out
        spaces,
Flapping to lesser shrubs outside their known comfort zones
As shafts of light long absorbed by the forgotten leaves that
        shielded us through the summer bathe our balcony and
        living room.

At twilight the chainsaw man returns;
Walking across the stumps and the grizzled deadwood he takes a
        small twig in his hands and tests how its still living texture
        bends with him and doesn't crack,
Instinctively he grabs his lower back as if he's put something out,
All the time the myna birds sing erratically for the end of day.

The King

by Michael O'Sullivan

Bulbous, bloated, dark leather brown,
The King stands alone on the fresh concrete
Of the Sha Kok Mei village-house veranda,
Chewing regurgitated cud,
Dunging up the builders' sand.
He's tasted it all before,
He could once tell saliva
From the warm grass-juice backwash
Flooding his system,
But those days are gone.

Sinewy, straitened, steamed chicken beige,
The bamboo workers catch some shade,
Otherwise they'd be running the King off
This reclaimed patch of real estate.

The King stands motionless,
Staring down his competition reflected in the French windows,
Admiring his bulk.
Then he remembers why he's here,
He's called back to the taste of his first grass,
The downy brush that caught his first fall,
As a bloody, light brown tangle of knees and hooves
When, in the midnight lull of the sleeping village
A lone streetlamp captured his furtive birthing.

He whinnied and bellowed to his clan
Not half an hour ago and still they do not come,
He'll wait them out in the dune of builder's sand
And taste the cud of congress and memory.
The space between obeisance and order is dark,
One day he was King and they awaited his call.
Still they do not come,
The afternoon sun is dipping and the protection
Of the shade has drawn about him like recognition.

The Green Heart

by Jason Eng Hun Lee

Day breaks
in the body's night.
There, inside my head
the tree speaks.

Come closer: can you hear it?
"The Tree Within", Octavio Paz

Here, no one listens to the rain,
its nourishing sibilances.

No butterfly flies between cars
threading tales of transformation.

No wind blows through streets
ferrying love messages between poplars

and no stone monument commemorates
the heart's condition.

Here, each tree comprises its own island,
and each man is his own castaway.

Yet I harbor a secret that none
shall take away from me -

in the will of wild murmurings
that break through wind, water, stone,

I shall never admit defeat
in the city's concrete sea

where no voice sounds in the deep
from the depths of traffic jams

and as the night solidifies and heaps
its heavy weight upon my soul

my green heart starts to thump within,
and will go on thumping,

and only I shall hear it sing.

Back to Main Age

by Jason S Polley

It's the question, the reason, the subject, the topic.
QRST
A
No
The

The

The aim goal mark quest

Poetry
Prosery
Prosody
Persnickety

It's the question, the object, the rub
Aye
Its question is question enough entire
That's the
The, the
The the.
Full stop

Wandering from sunset and -rise
Wondering from twilight to -light
Or is it twi-?

This, this, this thing, this thing just above, that this, that, this
       that, that that, I
Trickery
Just nitpickery trickery
Or, better, chicanery

With cheek
No
Audacity impudence sass
Edict of order ordering
Addictive order
Addict hoarder
Effront
Tarry
Tarry not

Facetious
AEIOU
Wherefore the sometimes why
Y
Facetiously
See see see

There, there, above, here, plummeting again into the quagmire
        of obfuscation
Quagmire of obfuscation

Enough

Quagmire of obfuscation
Gimme a

Smokescreen
Break

Fuck, the phrase
That phrase
That watchword above

Locution too is the name
Right
Wordwatch
Ob

Veracious
Dependable
Defensible
Unassailable
Saleable
All
Is

It
That that dictum
Mired
Copies what it condemns
Redoes what it decries
Duplicates what it deprecates
Duplicates what it deprecates

That morass muddying mystifica
Syllables
One two three four
That morass muddying ~~and~~ mystifying incredulity
One two three ~~one~~ ~~unseen one~~ four five

The rhyme, the iambs, the assonance, the association, the
        alliteration
Count count count
Error Error
Ass
The forced
Enjambment

Enjambment
Which I won't
En
Jamb
He, me, I eschew as I do
Or versa vice

The asininity
The asininity of the word asininity
The pomposity of the term pompous
Not unlike
Not unlike not unlike itself, as a matter of
Not unlike not unlike itself, as a matter
As

And the lasciviousness of lascivious
Particularly when enunciated
When
Ssss in lieu of shhh
Anglo angled

Articulated onanism

With onomatopoeia waiting to be spelled
Six six
Yes
A bee a bee a bee
A spell
ing

In lieu of rather than rather than or instead of instead of instead of
Above, I mean
Like notwithstanding instead of in spite of
Of of of
Oves oves oves

Dee-lessly
El-lessly
Unflown doves flued
Dead love
Zzz

The flu the flu
Of of of
Above above
The of of of
The
More buildings multiplying neogeometrically
Two four eight
The coasts pushed further and further away
Farther
Working further to push farther
Amassed mass amassed
Bivouacked
To the point where cement sighs
As the trees and seas longtired of chanting
Then canting
Slanting

Buildingsbuildingseveryallwhere
Jangajungledtogether
Mishmash ensemble
Hodgepodge pastiche
Bricks and bivouacs
Coughing cacophony
Attack
A lack
Surfaces hiding absent things
Municipal camouflage
Inner- and outerflage

Hibrowbeaten concealmentcontainment

And

And and and

The sea no longer sings
The sun retired
And the air
The air of
The air
heir
ear
err
of
Insert city name here
of Nezahualcoyotl

of
The air of
Hong Kong has been
p
o
i
s
o
n
e
d

Enough
No
Si
En verdad

For real
Claro
It's obvious
Es obvio

I, we, it
Cannot go on
Yau lok ah ng goi
I, we, it
Will go on

Silencing the sea
Handcuffing the sun
Engineering the obsolescence of shine

Of moonlight
Sun's sons numbed
Numbered
Noodles noodles

Demetaphysicalized demagoguery
Via brickery trickery slickery
By way of
As per
Gur
Bricks papier mached in upbeat concrete
And gleaming glass godless
Prison bars daffodiled
Pansy plastered
Daubed
Ob
Bb
Dd

Glass longing

Glass long longing longingly
For the white coasts black beaches from whence

From whence
Whence
It laughingly laid
Sand played
Sashayed

Retired and respired

Charmed
Coaxed
Cushioned
Cajoled

Pooled and passive
And was
And

As

Release from Darkness

by Rachna Joshi

Leo is in the ascendant in December,
when the Calgary Stampede is six months away.

In these moonlit prairie streets
the sugar moon is outside Younge Street Café.

Chasing me through these neon streets
are Valkyries hunting in the Arctic air.

In my dream your dark face advances
and clouds float around these panelled walls.

Magic beads, crystals and New Age books
nestle among the Tarot cards.

My mother prays and does the I-Ching for me -
"The Prince will be released from darkness today."

Rajasthan in the Rains

by Rachna Joshi

The temple in Nathdwara,
Gilded blue roofs amid
A sea of white marble.
The pigeons fly as
The priests scatter offerings -
Heavy, sugar-coated rotis.
Inside, Srinathji in repose
While the devout thunder
Through the doorways.
Pichhwai paintings
Line the lanes of the city.

Udaipur,
City of lakes,
Rain after five years.
In the city palace
We go past the Rana Pratap Gallery,
The women's quarters
And the cages for tigers.

It all ends in Chittorgarh
Where the history of Rajputana
Lies in the fort.
Padmini committing Jauhar
While hundreds of Rajput soldiers die
Dressed in women's clothes inside palanquins.
The Victory tower
With defaced sculptures
The Jain temples near
The Kirti stambh.

My Monkey Grammarian

by Trish Hopkinson

This search, this verbal trap of dread
and the ending unknown.
Is this path the poem - the journey
that dissolves into nothingness?
Is there anything after this narrow trail
of howling trees and screaming monkeys?
Is their rhetoric leading us
to nothing but language?
We are both fleeing and falling like footsteps,
devoured and created like fruit,
precarious and perfect like gravity,
like Galta abandoned.
We are driven by our own ceremonies,
by whirling words and dervish skeletons.
Our linguistic corruption stretches out
to the horizon and curves into the atmosphere,
a maze made of metaphors, stuffed in sacks
and piled in rows. Discourse itself, leaps
back and forth, and grammar leans in
to critique the universe
while the shadow of Splendor recites verse
more naked than herself. Her expressions
float into the evening like incense
from an altar in search of the end.

Inner Tree

by Andy Smerdon

Prune lightly my dear,
at the tree of my emotions
anchored deep within my core.
It may never recover,
from the savage secateurs
of your clear-cut anger.

Music of the Rain

by Sunil Sharma

in response to "Hear the rain"

And the rain slides down the
Window panes in liquid lines,
Finally terminating on the ground tiles,
Bubbling there in small glittering pools,
Dressed up in dark orange hues by the
Glowing sodium-vapor lamps, lining the
Deserted street and the freshly-washed tarmac
Exposed to the rough and playful masculine winds.
Are you hearing, the rain?

The rain is a murmur of syllables so claims Paz,
The man with an opened Inner Eye and talked of drifting time
In that marvelous ode to rain and a mysterious listener therein,
Talking of apparitions on a night earlier not seen.

The rain has got its own music - pitter-patter,
That is how we try to capture that natural rhythm
In words and syntax not meant to resemble those
Divine sounds.

I see faces floating up before the open casements
Long-buried in time,
Faces familiar/forgotten
Carried by the water-air
Driven by the roaring wind.
Time collapses in that single moment
Past/present collide,
A mist rises off the distant river,
And I hear a loud distant hoot
Of a truck on the glistening highway,
I must now sleep,
It is 3 am and I have to catch
the 7:30 am train!

Pauses in Transit

by Mags Webster

after "Between going and staying"

Across the city, elevators
rise like bubbles to the rim
of a glass. Descent
is condensation. The sky,
a tension plugged
with cloud, sweats
surface onto rivulets
of steel, slicks
the wickerwork
of scaffolding.
On a concrete
cliff, a butterfly
alights, spreads
a tiny book
of papery wings,
makes a poem
on an opaque wall,
thirty-nine storeys high.

You Voyage My Body...

by Mags Webster

after "Sun stone"

... surf cirrostratus
past hidden eclipses
blood-din of moon
electric disturbance
swim east in search
of a mythical sun
a petalled corona
preparing for solstice
there is no star cluster
to show you the way
only my body
its currents and craving
you carry your fire
right into the flood
drown in the dark
ocean world of me
your comet tail
writhing with light.

Durham, 1980

by Marjorie Becker

in memory of Octavio Paz

Madrid, 1937: the heart
of Paz's "Sun Stone" -
a man, a woman melding against hard earth,
naked against a plaza known in peace for incandescent coffee.
In '37 Paz's woman,
and his man worked against,
worked through time,
only language's shards,
only love,
and the Nazis used Spain to test their will,
while Paz's woman,
his man, loved open,
loved as if
no
body.

Then Dan said, "Woman,"
he said "woman,
you teach me Paz by Durham night.
You feed me membrillo, work the quince paste
against hardening scrolls of bread,
your small hands fill my mouth.
We move toward fire,
I enter you on your floor,
this is not me,
the real me roams Israel,
your hands, they work my legs,
I take you to the bed,
this is not me, I never display,
and anyway, this is secondary,

I never allow,
but the taste of pomegranate between your legs,
I am weak above you,
your hands, they smell of pine,
your hands with golden spikes,
your hands are water,
today I'm someone else,
I count, I count your hours
push you toward a center,
work your legs like corn meal,
whoever else you've loved,
whatever I've pretended,
I think to make you new
know to make you me."

After I left you, Dan,
you prowled my diaries,
their tangled scratches,
coded allusions to another man,
to a man who liked my raw music, my helpless grunts.
You read them as denial:
what if Madrid '37 wasn't,
what if the woman opened her arms to a scavenger,
took his handful of wisteria pods filled with secret words,
what if Paz was wrong,
no Spanish Republicans,
no man on the plaza,
only a woman,
her open tongue a morgue.

Aging
by S Mickey Lin

after "Between going and staying"

Aging,
I look to the horizon,
Clouds of confusion.

The deadline looms near,
Borders are drawn,
The forked road remains.

To genuflect home,
Crawl back to infancy,
Poisons my soul.

To stand proud,
Satiate my pride,
Starves my body.

Ambitions of the spirit,
Necessities of the flesh,
Cast shadows over my mind.

I lie in a drunken state,
Neither asleep nor awake,
Just *being*.

Human and being,
Billions of atoms colliding within,
Dying.

You, My Whispering Ilex Tree

by Ciriaco Offeddu

My grandfather traced a yard barely bigger than your boughs,
And erected this wintry house respecting you and the view of
    Mughina Gorge.
He was capable of acts of love, never of words.
And you repay that lost sentiment: you are my brother and my
    pet, my confessor,
And my clown too.
Protected by the walls, and yet you move with the storm,
    exaggerating its effects.
I know you play with me and tease me swaying your fronds
    during the nights,
Groaning and howling, as if you were a lad.
I like the after-dawn, when the light of the valley is neat,
And the air from the convent of the Jesuits is thin and scented.
There is silence.
And you, looking ahead, relieve your bloom and sigh.
I'm fond of the rain, when it falls softly without wind.
You'd have a calm shower and finally relax pouring small clouds
    from your bark, happily.
I hug you while the notes of the drops are toning down,
And I feel your slow pulse:
"You are only ten," you say, "and many things will become clear
    later in time.
Her death too."
I do not have the faculty to argue.
I'll content myself with the quiet: my fears are full of voices more
    and more petulant,
And nobody breaks them up.

Queen Among Leaves

by Judy Keung

On a granite wall you stretch,
scarlet brown, greenish red,
like a silent flame you spread,
waxy and soft, tender and strong.
apple green framed by rustic red.

You open your palms,
your veins translucent arteries,
You expose your neck,
daring yet vulnerable.
You creep, you crawl, you cling.

Queen among leaves,
quiet conqueror,
unafraid of icy scorn,
proud to be you,
not eye-catching

till you show your true colors.

Tall Tree in the Ear

by Hao Guang Tse

after "Árbol adentro"

Tall tree in the ear
gardened by God -
when you burst this brittle
pot, will I, now broken,
learn how to listen, to
lie face down,
bury my head in the richest
earth, and, mouth
full, go praising
each fruit?

This is Not Home

by Melanie Ho

after "Between going and staying"

1.

We tell stories:
I'm here to find my roots and long-lost relatives.
As if I can hike up a hill and pull some grass
walk past a table at dim sum and say,
you've got black hair. Come with me.
You'll never find them
                say the believers
as if I've been looking
as if I know where and how and why to search.
Ah! You want to find home.
Ah, I reply. Where I'm from there's no word for home.

2.

As the years bleed into each other
I count the cycles of friends who've arrived and departed
(two times three is six)
and now I'm dancing with a third:
on Tuesday nights we run the Twins, searching for clarity
or that overrated inner peace
and detox and retox and detox again.
It's a fortune cookie that tells me to stop:
                what's good
is already gone.

3.
We're awake and asleep
the jetlag lingers, refusing to depart.
How long have you been here? asks a taxi driver.
A row of grinning bobbleheads
teases from the dashboard.
Seven years:
I'm still living between time zones.

Morning

by Melanie Ho

after "Árbol adentro" - "A tree within"

Come: watch as the leaves
shake off the night's rain.
Inhale: let the air travel down your spine.
Reveille takes place at six.
I had forgotten what it's like
to stand atop a hill and look onto a panorama
too striking to photograph
and burn the edges or tint with warm purple.
For once, keep a secret: do not hash tag this.
Do you remember the 90s trend of noses
blending oils to synthesize
autumn leaves and spring grass, ocean waves
air.
Remind me: what does a dream smell like?
We've stood here before
alongside trees whose limbs
shoot out in all directions,
too old, too strong to tremble in the wind.
After slipping on smooth stones,
stand up again and fill your diaphragm.
There's not much
of this rosemary and lavender air left.

Poetry Speaks

by Joy Al-Sofi

after "The word outloud"

Spellbound
words stumble.
Capture, twist
a spider scrawls
bent to our bidding
splayed on a page.
Words like a phoenix rise
memory's invisible worlds
scoop a sarcophagus of time
inside us
we are becoming language
language inside us
is becoming
us.
What we name,
we think
we own.

Can You Hear Me?

by Luisa A. Igloria

after "Hear the rain - Como quien oye llover"

Is this a good connection?
I have a little over an hour
on my cellphone load.
The rain in Hong Kong
is not like the rain in Baguio,
where we used to live.
The fog sometimes
might remind me.
Or the hills when I have time
to take a Sunday walk.
I like to walk by myself
especially in a drizzle.
Just a little rain feels refreshing.
When the mist veils my face
I feel most homesick.
How old is your baby, the one
I used to take care of?
I remember I helped you
take her home from the hospital
in the pouring rain.
You nearly slipped
when you came out of the car,
but I steadied your elbow.
I have no children of my own.
I think about her and count the years.
She is a young woman now, all grown.
I remain unmarried
but the years are mostly kind.
Or they are shifty like the light
that glances off the harbor.

From the ferry I see bands of neon,
the bright signs and the flash of cars
passing on the highway.
My current employers are kind.
Here, we know it isn't
always so. So many other girls
and women like me are tempted
by the exit signs they imagine
written above high-rise windows.
The tarmac is a launch pad
for some dreams that never return.
I consider myself lucky.
The man, he stays
most days in a room
looking at old films.
The first time I heard his voice
on the TV screen I blinked.
When he was younger,
he used to be an actor.
His wife, she eats nothing
but vegetables. She likes
for me to prepare everything fresh.
She sells tea. They sit in fragrant
packets in boxes along the hall.
We also live in a high-rise apartment.
There is a balcony where I am allowed
to hang some things: damp towels,
dish cloths. They let me keep a plant
and I water it there. When it rains,
I close the balcony door carefully.
I watch the water streak
the windowpanes.

When I go to church I look
for the font of holy water.
Coming and going I dip
my fingers and cross myself.
Do you remember
how young I was when first
I joined your household?
It was the season of monsoon.
I had one bag of belongings,
I had nowhere else really
to go. I rose at six to boil
the children's bath water,
and the water for coffee and tea.
I laid the plates and the silver,
warmed the bread, boiled the eggs.
The seasons turn from one
to the other. I used to sing
while I cooked but someone
told me that might bring a storm.
After the dishes were done
I did the laundry at the tap
beside the back steps.
The smell of soap, the suds
that swirled in the dull
silver basin - who knew
how much water could fill
a pocket or a sleeve?
I hope to see you again
some day soon. I could tell you
stories. All this time, you are
almost kin to me: not
this shore still so oddly
distant, its hems an island
circled with water and rain.

A Lover, Who is About to Leave

by Sreya Mallika Datta

and you were a pause as you
turned to look back
at the world growing small
in the palm of my hand,
but soon spreading,
thinly, thinly,
like films of sunlight on ocean waves,
like the lines of my palm,
struggling to get across and fall over
its sinewy edge, but
wavering, faltering.

the world sinks.
swirls, dives,
in your measured pause
(your poised pause, I almost feel like saying!)
the world, my world
trails behind you
like the veil of hair
that dances in the wind.

between going and staying
you come to my doorstep,
and I look across for a final reprieve,
but you, you are frozen in a pause,
for, having left,
you do not leave.

Spode

by Shahilla Shariff

I

He loved but from a distance.
There was a strange perfection in that.
He imagined me pouring tea
so he had it wrapped,
the two-cup bone china teapot
its wispy carnation drawing,
luminous line of opal spout.
That was how I came to sip tea
as he wrestled memory in his sleep.

II

She died last night,
exactly as she feared
languishing for days until the cleaner came.
The carpet stained with tea,
a cup overturned, a teabag limp
at saucer's edge, her tiny frame slumped
into the worn comfort of prayer beads,
her dream of Africa,
facing the bareness of wintered trees.

III

I take my tea each day from a similar cup.
Spode. One of a set. One-of-a-kind. Specially commissioned.
The red splotched guinea fowl looking freshly hand-painted
despite the sixty odd years in between.
More than the cup, an intimation
of long darkness broken,
familiar patterns of deepening afternoon,
unmistakeable rituals of the living
all the while as we commemorate the dead.

Lost Summers

by Shahilla Shariff

The lilacs at least were free.
Huge bunches snapped
off branches, the profuse greenness
of summer flowering trees.
The mauves and whites quivering,
stalks suspended in a glass jar.
Indoors, they seemed lost,
but for us, solace in the scent
of sheer abandon billowing
into still, dank days.

Emerald City Blues

by Phoebe Tsang

Forty percent of the city is green!
Behind her the ziggurat-spine
of mountains was cascading
down to Kowloon Harbour where
a small girl posed for her photo
beside Bruce Lee - he'd been standing
so long in the midday sun
his skin had blackened to bronze.
I saw no plaque on his plinth,
he didn't need one.
No junks in the water, no more
red paper sails webbed like dragons' tails.

On the far shore, glass-eyed monoliths glared
behind a blue-grey curtain of smog.
The view from our sixteenth-floor
restaurant was clear, flecked
with treetops like clusters
of Swarovski crystals dyed
the color of emeralds -
impressive, without the cost.

My hilltop-dwelling friend was happy
as a bird here; over lunch she sang
the praises of parks and hiking trails
backed by the verdant
vista unfurled at the window.
It was my first day in Hong Kong
and I was in love with the aerial view
I'd drifted down into just
hours ago, past mountains
lush as giant leaf-clad breasts.

That day, I hadn't yet journeyed to the glass
heart of the Emerald City and seen
Dorothy curtseying before a life-size statue
surrounded by souvenir shops.
Maybe it was the weather - forty degrees
on the boardwalk, sweating in my jeans -
even with my tinted glasses,
I couldn't make out a hint of green
through the poisoned mists.

It's been eighteen years since
I last saw my hometown
but now that I've crossed the Pacific
and docked in her harbor,
all I'd ask of the great Oz
is to take us back to the forest.

Going Home
by Phoebe Tsang

At dawn, the carts glistened with wet scales
as if the fish were still alive,
not drowning for lack of water.
They slept just like the rest of us,
breathed city air.
As the sun rose, the glitter faded from their gills.
By noon, the last dregs were fins and bones
kicked to the gutter,
entrails slick under fishermen's boots.
The fishermen gone home,
back to the sea.

In Search of Validation
by Sylvia Riojas Vaughn

    after "Proem"

Odd that I, child of the Spanish conquest of Tenochtitlán, speak
English. I look to Shakespeare for poetry, drama. Paz, you peek
into Plato's cave at inspiration's fire, clip pronouns in the garden
of Epicurus. Our Mexican ancestors uttered sounds of love,
betrayal, anguish, none exclusive to the ancients. Illuminate the
world with your native song, strew marigolds and roses from the
gardens of your people.

Poetic Justice

by Jun Pang

poetry is the anathema of poetry
is perennial - poetry is pallid
Pythagorean perfection,
righting wrongs and
wronging writers
from forever ago.
poetry is running in circles
and running away from the monochrome embrace
of prosaic punctuation;
poetry is human multiplicity, the urban abode of the just
and the well-versed,
a de-
vice of Romantic proportions.
poetry trails over the trajectory of bro-
ken promises
and smothers solitude
with slow, swooning swan song melodies;
poetry is, against the sanctity of
straight syntax, sin.
poetry is a nesting ground
for severed linguistic roots,
but poetry roots out
empirical prefixes
and pretension,
prickling at the silence
of inane imprecations.
poetry is mistaking misgivings
about nouns and verbs
for vivid illusions of
stranger words and stranger worlds -
poetry walks a mile in our shoes
only to walk a thousand more

in search of better souls.
poetry dares to eat a peach
but poetry doesn't dare repeat
the fulsome frivolities
of forever ago:
poetry
is catharsis is
poetry
is poeisis is
poetry
is poetry is
poetry.

When the Rainbow Graced the Sky

by Paola Caronni

The rain abandoned its sheet of glaze
taking with it the mist, the drizzle, the steam
and you.

The sky boasts now a waterfall of colors,
a palette of feelings.
I move towards the closed window, still wet from the storm,
taking a long look at the greenery besides the approaching darkness.
It was there, where I perceived the gentle step of a flower.
The rain brought the storm
within myself and in the clouds above
after you crossed that road,
and stepped into my head.
Time and sorrow disappeared like in a cloudless night,
droplets of joy heated my heart,
steam of pleasure possessed my aching body
in a carousel of give and take.
The window, scarcely scared by the banging panels,
shuts down suddenly,
as you stop talking and listening to the joy of the dripping rain.
And to me.
As you exit from the main door.
Your hair abandons my pillow,
your body leaves a mark on the bed sheet,
the years, months and days
mutter words of ice.
The cascading colors flash their beauty to the dying day.
The terrace is an empty space that cradles my aching soul.
Your beauty is frozen in time,
forever whispering the words of the rain,
as a magic spell.

Poetry as Religion
by Kirpal Singh

for Octavio Paz

Reading an invitation to write a poem (or two) about you
I remembered our brief but memorable meeting -
1972 - was it? Mexico City? Somewhere, memory fails
But the siren, like the seashell, remains fully alive
Inviting children of the mire, poverty and more
To celebrate what you always said was our salvation -
Poetry, the secret religion, your passion and your pain.

Between the stone and the flower stand japan, india
Buddhism and noh, machado and lawrence (DH), eliot
The hungry generation who needed you to inspire
Give strength, courage, testament to idelology
Even as you diplomatically weaved and wove and spun
Word after word after word, defying, resisting, fighting
For you knew that conscience makes cowards of us all.

In the alternating current of global politics galore
You sounded a language of forceful persuasion
As you painted and drew image after image after image
Challenging us all to think and rethink what we do, did
With the wild moon as our witness, eagle and sun
Convergences, disjunctions and conjunctions, poems
That make the bow and the lyre move mountains
Into the valleys you so loved and admired and made your

Paz, all the awards and the glories meant little to you
But for their power to arrest the world's attention
And bring us all closer to what you always warned -
The curse of modernization, the death of feeling
And the impossible mating of poetry and humanity.

101

Age

by Agnès Bun

to Octavio Paz - to my Grandfather

The veins on his arms
Like dry roots on an old tree
Roads on the map of a life
About to be forgotten

For a long time
He was an oak
Tall and dignified
Almighty
Always there
And always will be

He toured the world
Drunk on solitude
A suitcase for a home
Carrying the same loneliness
A heaviness
Spoken in several languages
Crossing many bridges
Over the same turbulent waters
Just different oceans
Child of the sea

His life
An open wound
With no stitches

These legs that took him everywhere
Today they are thin and dry
Frozen
He, once almighty
Now so tiny
His white hair crowning
The shadow of a soul
Always there
But that will soon cease to be

O child of the sea
You have washed up on the shore
Leaving faint steps in the sand
Already erased by the wind
the waves
the world
you left behind

Sometimes the sparkle of a thought
Fireworks lighting up the sky
But soon the night falls on his eyes
again
Those shiny eyes
Before burning with curiosity
Before burning with worlds inside
Now stillborn stories
Now unlit candles

This tree cannot bear fruits anymore
One by one its leaves are falling
With each word he dies a little
All that is left
Is the language of his bones

He sits there
A compass without a North
Pointing towards every direction
And not seeing them
Lost
Trapped
In a labyrinth of solitude
In a body
full of
anonymous memories

His cold hands grip mine
Just a spasm
And I
Hating every minute apart
Dreading every minute together
Look at him
And think
Hope
That he is free

One day the tree
Collapses
It is the cruellest moment
When it falls down
As it cannot feel its own roots anymore
Collapses
Dying,
Dying;
Dead.

Now children pick up your leaves on the ground
And I can still hear your voice
In the laughter of kids
In the whispers of the wind
Laughing at death
At peace in a world finally yours
A traveler in life
A wanderer in death
A page torn forever
From an old book
Written by the stars
I still carry in my bag.

The Last Days of Octavio Paz

by Wang Jiaxin, translated by Diana Shi and George O'Connell

Mexico City, dusk,
his eyes wide
as a great conflagration
devours his house, his life's
possessions, the years
of manuscripts, poems finished
and unfinished, the Aztec mask,
the Picasso, chairs
of his ancestors, photos from childhood,
the joyous dome, its ribbed beams and rafters,
everything turning to ash
in a whirling column of fire.

The flames blaze on,
charring night,
lick the black wings
soaring from his poems,
consume the leaden hours,
human illusion, human desire,
wish and ambition,
emptiness and ash -
all crackling in a fire
come late in life,
as firemen shout in the choking dark,
fleeting shadows.

So late, so late
but now set free
from long affliction,
Octavio Paz will sit once more
beside a Paris street,
dry leaves scuttling silent at his feet,
a far off light
dawning on his brow.

Acknowledgments

Our deep appreciation to the poets who have generously contributed to this book. Their voices, both distinct and distinctive, have made this conversation richer. We would also like to thank Peter Gordon, whose knowledge and affection for Spanish literature on both sides of the Atlantic were providential. And to David McKirdy, for his support and encouragement from the first days of the idea. They have all made possible this unique experience.

Afterword

WE DECIDED TO provide a selection of Octavio Paz's poems as a starting point for this "conversation". Limiting ourselves to only a few proved very difficult, however, for Octavio Paz wrote such a large number of accomplished poems. While much of his work is imbued with profound meaning, cultural references and literary allusions, his mastery of the form is also reflected in poems of lighthearted sensibility.

The eight poems we ended up selecting* are among Paz's best known and are, we think, representative of his wide range of moods and sentiments, ideal for those previously unacquainted with him or the topics of his poems. They were intended to spark inspiration and also to sow seeds of greater curiosity.

~ 0 ~

In "Piedra de sol"—or "Sun Stone"—Paz reaches the pinnacle of artistic and poetic expression. It is now considered the foundation of his oeuvre and one of the most important poems of the twentieth century. It begins with these justly celebrated first lines:

> *un sauce de cristal, un chopo de agua,*
> *un alto surtidor que el viento arquea,*
> *un árbol bien plantado mas danzante,*
> *un caminar de río que se curva,*
> *avanza, retrocede, da un rodeo*
> *y llega siempre*

> a crystal willow, an aqueous poplar,
> a high fountain arching in the wind,
> a well-rooted tree that's dancing,
> a waterway that curves,
> advances, retreats, detours
> and yet arrives

A long poem, 584 lines of eleven syllables each, the circular "Piedra de sol" marks the Aztec calendar, starting where it ends and ending where it begins. While the poem makes mention of, among others, Dante, Christian imagery, Greek mythology, Lincoln, Madero, Trotsky, and the Spanish Civil War, as well as to love and memory, Paz also ponders on some basic questions about life and our existence:

> ¿la vida, cuándo fue de veras nuestra?,
> ¿cuándo somos de veras lo que somos?

> Life, when was it truly ours?
> When are we truly what we are?

The poem—like much modernist poetry—can be dense and difficult, but it is characteristic of Paz that every poem can be read and enjoyed at many levels and by people with different levels of familiarity with his poetic and cultural references, for Paz also cared deeply about rhythm and musicality, and was fully aware of the expressive possibilities of words and the emotions they help kindle.

The spoken and written word, language, poetry and the art of poetry, are common themes—themes and concerns Paz shared with his fellow poets and hence obvious choices to begin this conversation; we include two that show this most explicitly:

The word outloud (*La palabra dicha*)
The word arises
written from the page.
The word,
stalactitic,
on a column engraved
letter by letter one by one.
Its echo icing over
the stony sheet.

Essence,
white like the page,
the word arises.
It walks
the high-wire
from silence to shout
on the edge
of strictly saying.
Hearing: sound's nest,
its labyrinth.

What it says it says not
what it says: how to say
what it says not?
                              Say
perhaps the virgin is urgent.

A cry
in a dead crater
in another galaxy
how does one say ataraxy?

What is said is said
straight and backwards
the mind demined
of mine off-line
cemetery, some tarry
seamen's no semen.

Ear's labyrinth
what you say is un-said
from silence to shout
unheard.

Innocence in no sense:
Shut up to speak.

"The word outloud" is a poet's poem, for poetry is both a written and spoken form; here Paz contrasts and merges the two. *"Proema"*, or "Proem", is literally a prose poem, a commingling of the two forms:

Proem *(Proema)*
At times poetry is the vertigo of bodies and the vertigo of
      speech and the vertigo of death;
walking, eyes closed, along the edge of the precipice and the
      verbena of underwater gardens;
the laugh that sets fire to rules and holy commandments;
the parachute descent of words onto the beaches of the
      page;
the despair that embarks on a paper boat and crosses,
for forty nights and forty days, the sea of nocturnal anguish
and the rock-strewn terrain of daytime anguish;
the idolatry of "I" and the dissipation of "I";
the beheading of epithets, the burying of mirrors;
the recollection of freshly cut pronouns in the gardens of
      Epicurus and Nezahualcoyotl;
the flute solo on the terrace of memory and the dance of
      flames in the caverns of thought;
the migrations of flocks of verbs, wings and claws, seeds and
      hands;
the bony and root-laden nouns planted in the undulations of
      language;
love unseen and love unheard and love unspoken:
love to love.

But some of Paz's poems touch us more directly. Paz frequently recited these at academic and popular forums, and on the radio and television. One of his favorites—and it is easy to see why—is *"Como quien oye llover"*:

Hear the rain (*Como quien oye llover*)
Hear me as you hear the rain,
in the back of your mind,
pitter-patter, drizzling,
water that is air, air that is time,
the day's not yet gone,
evening's yet to come,
figures in the mist,
just 'round the corner,
figures of time,
at the bend in this moment,
hear me as you hear the rain,
without hearing, but hearing what I say,
with eyes open to what's within,
asleep with the senses awake,
it's raining, pitter-patter, a murmur of syllables,
air and water, weightless words:
of what we were and are,
the days and years, this moment,
time without weight, enormous burden,
hear me as you hear the rain,
the wet tarmac shining,
the mist rises and walks,
the night opens and watches me,
it's you wrapped in mist,
you and your face of night,
you and your skin, faintly flashing,
crossing the street, entering by my temples,
watery paces on my eyelids
hear me as you hear the rain,
the tarmac glistens, you cross the street,
it's the wandering fog in the night,
it's the night asleep in your bed,
it's the ocean swell of your breathing,
your watery fingers wet my brow,

your fiery fingers burn my eyes,
your airy fingers open the eyelids of time,
gushing forth apparitions and resurrections,
hear me as you hear the rain,
the years pass, the moments return,
can you hear your steps next door?
neither here nor there: you hear them
in another time that is right now,
hear the steps of time,
creator of places without mass or location,
hear the rain running down the terrace,
the night is already darker in the copse,
the rays have bedded down among the leaves,
a rambling garden adrift
—come, your shadow covers this page.

One can hear his voice here in this poem that never ceases
to awake the wisp of a smile. A similar yet shorter poem—and
one of the clear favorites among the poets contributing to this
collection—is "Entre irse y quedarse":

Between going and staying (*Entre irse y quedarse*)
Between going and staying, the day is stuck,
a block of frozen transparency.

Everything is seen yet all is elusive:
the horizon untouchably near.

Papers on the table, a book, a vase:
all rest in the shadow of their names.

Blood ascends more slowly through my veins
a single syllable beating stubbornly in my temples.

The indifferent light transforms
opaque walls, time without history.

114

The afternoon has spread out: now it's a bay
rocking the world with its gentle swaying.

We are neither asleep nor awake:
We are, we just are.

The moment lets itself go:
we pull ourselves away; pauses in transit.

Reality for Paz is not something solid, but rather something that only exists when experienced and can only be experienced through the medium of the senses, filtered by both the conscious and unconscious.

Paz can be very direct and very laconic: some poems are very short. We included some of these here. "Hermandad" or "Brotherhood" is partially based on verses attributed to the astronomer Claudius Ptolemy reflecting Platonic ideas of the immortality of the soul and the divinity: who, he asks, plays with us?

Brotherhood (Hermandad: homenaje a Claudio Ptolomeo)
I am man; how little I last
and the night stretches on.
But I look toward the sky:
the stars are writing.
Without comprehending, I understand:
I am also written,
and at this very moment
someone is noting me down.

"*Madrugada*" is very short and to the point:

Dawn (*Madrugada*)
Cold quick hands
one by one pull back
the bands of darkness
I open my eyes
    I remain
alive
    in the middle
of a wound still fresh.

Our final selection is "Árbol adentro" or "A tree within",
which was included in the book of poems of the same title. It
shows Paz's control of metaphor, here with powerful and Surrealist
imagery.

A tree within (*Árbol adentro*)
A tree's grown inwards
from my temples.
Veins are its roots
nerves its branches
and thoughts its tangle of leaves.
Your glances ignite it
and its shaded fruits
are blood oranges
and pomegranates of flame.

Day breaks
in the body's night.
There, inside my head
the tree speaks.

Come closer: can you hear it?

It ends, like so much of Paz's poetry, with an invitation to the reader to "come closer" and listen. The editors are gratified that so many poets from Hong Kong, Asia and beyond accepted this invitation.

---

* Although accomplished translations of all these poems can be found in *The Collected Poems of Octavio Paz: 1957-1987*, edited and translated by Eliot Weinberger (New Directions, 1991), we decided—as part of the process of presenting these selected poems to Asian poets—to translate them ourselves, in whole or (in the case of *"Piedra de sol"*), in part. Peter Gordon executed these translations, reproduced here. But we wish to acknowledge the use of Weinberger's translations as references; certain similarities are inevitable.

Contributors

Gémino H. Abad, University Professor emeritus of literature and creative writing at the University of the Philippines, is a poet, fictionist, literary critic and historian, with various honors and awards.

Michellan Alagao is a mother, freelance writer and anti-human trafficking advocate. She currently works at a global organization that seeks to protect the poor from violence.

Joy Al-Sofi is a published poet who has taught English in Hong Kong since 2004. A member of the Hong Kong Writers Circle, she is finishing her MFA at City University of Hong Kong.

José Ángel Araguz is a Mexican-American poet. A CantoMundo fellow, he runs the poetry blog *The Friday Influence* (where more of his work can be found) at *thefridayinfuence.wordpress.com*

Isabela Banzon teaches and heads the creative writing program at the University of the Philippines.

Marjorie Becker is the author of the forthcoming *Dancing on the Sun Stone: An Exploration of Mexican Women and the Gendered Politics of Octavio Paz.*

Agnès Bun is a French journalist in Hong Kong of Sino-Cambodian extraction. She won the 2010 Daniel Pearl Award and has reported on unrest in Ukraine and Typhoon Haiyan in the Philippines.

Paola Caronni has a degree in English Language and Literature from the State University in Milan; her thesis focused on Hong Kong. A tutor of Italian, translator and poet, she has lived in Hong Kong since 1995.

Sreya Mallika Datta is from Kolkata. Her writings have appeared in such publications as the *Sahitya Akademi Bi-monthly Journal* and the *Inspired By* series launched by the British Council and Sampad South Asian Arts.

Kit Fan is a Hong Kong poet, now living in the UK. His first book of poems *Paper Scissors Stone* (2011) won the 2010 inaugural HKU International Poetry Prize.

Peter Gordon is publisher at Chameleon Press and editor of *The Asian Review of Books.*

Louise Ho is, after more than thirty years of writing, widely considered the doyenne of Hong Kong English-language literature. Her works are collected in *Incense Tree* (2009).

Melanie Ho (*melanie-ho.com*) is a writer from Ottawa, Canada. She has been living in Hong Kong since 2007.

Tammy Ho Lai-Ming (*sighming.com*) is founding co-editor of *Asian Cha* and Assistant Professor at Hong Kong Baptist University, where she teaches poetry, fiction and modern drama.

Trish Hopkinson (*trishhopkinson.com*) has been published in several journals, including *The Found Poetry Review* and *Chagrin River Review*. She resides in Utah with her husband and two children.

Luisa A. Igloria (*luisaigloria.com*) is the author of *Ode to the Heart Smaller than a Pencil Eraser*, winner of the 2014 May Swenson Prize, and twelve other books.

Rachna Joshi did her post-graduation in Creative Writing at Syracuse University. *Travel Tapestry* (2013) is her third volume of poetry, following *Configurations* (1993) and *Crossing the Vaitarani* (2008).

Timothy Kaiser is a Hong Kong poet, principal of the Upper School, Canadian International School of Hong Kong and author of the poetry collection *Food Court* (2003).

Kit Kelen, scholar, painter and poet, is Professor of English at the University of Macau. The most recent of his English-language poetry volumes is *China Years - New and Selected Poems*.

Judy Keung was born and bred in Hong Kong. Her first poetry collection is *Footprints and other poems* (2005); she has also been published in *Prairie Schooner*, *Becoming Poets* and elsewhere.

Agnes S. L. Lam was a Professor at the University of Hong Kong. Her publications include *A Pond in the Sky* (2013) and *Becoming Poets: The Asian English Experience* (2014).

Elbert Siu Ping Lee teaches psychology at Upper Iowa University, Hong Kong campus. His recent work can be found in the collection *Rain on the Pacific Coast* (2013).

Jason Eng Hun Lee helps co-ordinate poetry events in Hong Kong and was a finalist for the Melita Hume Award (2012). He teaches at Hong Kong Baptist University.

S. Mickey Lin (*mickeylin.com*) is a writer who splits his time between Southeast Asia and America. He regularly visits Hong Kong for dim sum and inspirations.

Dino Mahoney is a Lecturer in creative writing at the University of Hong Kong, formerly an RTHK writer/presenter, SCMP theatre critic & City University of Hong Kong Associate Professor.

Aaron Maniam is a Singapore poet whose work has been featured in collections in the USA, Australia and France. His collection *Morning at Memory's Border* was shortlisted for the 2007 Singapore Literature Prize.

David McKirdy is a poet from Hong Kong and the author of *Accidental Occidental* (recipient of an Arts Development Council grant in 2005 and reissued in 2011) and, most recently, *Ancestral Worship* (2014).

Reid Mitchell is a New Orleanian who has taught in China for many years. He has served as an editor for both *Asian Cha* and *Asia Literary Review.*

Juan José Morales is a Spanish lawyer and a former Chairman of the Spanish Chamber of Commerce in Hong Kong. He is also a regular contributor to *The Asian Review of Books.*

Germán Muñoz is a Mexican attorney and journalist. He has been president of the Mexican Chamber of Commerce in Hong Kong since 2013.

Collier Nogues (*colliernogues.com*) is the author of *On the Other Side, Blue: Poems*. She lives in Hong Kong, where she teaches creative writing and co-curates the Ragged Claws craft talk series.

George O'Connell is an award-winning American poet, translator, editor, creative writing and literature professor. With Diana Shi, he co-directs Hong Kong's Pangolin House (*pangolinhouse.com*).

Ciriaco Offeddu (*ciriacoffeddu.com*), an engineer and erstwhile CEO, has recently received an MFA in Creative Writing from City University of Hong Kong.

Michael O'Sullivan teaches at the Chinese University of Hong Kong and has lived in Hong Kong for six years. His previous books include *Weakness* and *The Incarnation of Language*.

Jun Pang was born and raised in Hong Kong, and is currently a Grade 12 student at the Canadian International School. "Poetic Justice" is her first published work.

Jason S Polley is Associate Professor of contemporary fiction at Hong Kong Baptist University, where he's toiled since 2007. He is the author of three books, including *Refrain* (2010) and *Cemetery Miss You* (2011).

Mani Rao (*manirao.com*) moved from India to Hong Kong in 1993. Her books include *Ghostmasters* (2010) and a translation of the Sanskrit Bhagavad Gita.

Danton Remoto is currently a Radio/TV producer in Manila. He is the author of three books of poems: *Skin Voices Faces*, *Black Silk Pajamas*, and *Honeymoon: The Love Poems*.

Page Richards is Associate Professor at the University of Hong Kong. She directs the MFA in Creative Writing, including the new Creative Writing Studio, and co-produces new Hong Kong drama.

Sylvia Riojas Vaughn (*dallaspoetscom.org/Vaughnbio.htm*) belongs to the Dallas Poets Community. Her work appears in the anthology *Bridge of Fates*.

Douglas Robinson is a writer, translator, translation scholar, and administrator at Hong Kong Baptist University.

Kate Rogers's last collection was *City of Stairs* (2012); her next, *Foreign Skin*, will debut in Toronto in 2015. She co-edited the *OutLoud Too* anthology (2014) and *Not a Muse: The Inner Lives of Women* (2009).

Shahilla Shariff's first poetry collection is *Life Lines* (2012). She was born in Kenya and is Canadian. A lawyer, she has lived in Hong Kong since 1993.

Sunil Sharma, based in Mumbai, is a widely-published poet, writer, critic, editor and interviewer. He is a college principal by profession and has published three collections of poetry and one of short fiction.

James Shea is the author of *Star in the Eye* and the forthcoming collection, *The Lost Novel*. He teaches in the Department of Humanities and Creative Writing at Hong Kong Baptist University.

Diana Shi is a literary editor, essayist and a translator of Chinese and American poetry. She co-directs Hong Kong's Pangolin House (*pangolinhouse.com*).

Kirpal Singh is currently director of the Wee Kim Wee Center at the Singapore Management University where he also teaches Creative Writing. He is the author of *Thinking Hat & Coloured Turbans* (2003).

Madeleine Slavick, a permaent resident of Hong Kong, is the author of several books of poetry, photography, and non-fiction. Her most recent book is *Fifty Stories Fifty Images* (2012).

Andy Smerdon was born in England, completed his schooling in Singapore and now lives in a small country town in Queensland, Australia. He writes poetry for the simple pleasure of doing so.

Tim Suermondt is the author of two full-length books of poems, the latest: *Just Beautiful* (2010). He loves the Star Ferry and could ride it all day.

Eddie Tay is Associate Professor at the Chinese University of Hong Kong and the reviews editor of *Asian Cha*. He is the author of three poetry collections and winner of the Singapore Literature Prize 2012 (English Category).

Phoebe Tsang (*phoebetsang.com*) is a British-Canadian poet, librettist and short story writer. Originally from Hong Kong, her poetry collection is *Contents of a Mermaid's Purse* (2009).

Hao Guang Tse (*vituperation.wordpress.com*) is interested in form and formation, creativity and quotation, lyrics and line breaks. The author of chapbook *hyperlinkage* (2013), he is working on a full-length collection.

Wang Jiaxin is an eminent contemporary Chinese poet, essayist, and translator. He serves as Professor of Chinese and Director of the International Writing Center at Renmin University, Beijing.

Mags Webster (*www.magswebster.com*), based in Hong Kong since 2011, is currently completing an MFA at City University. Her first poetry collection, *The Weather of Tongues* (2011), won Australia's Anne Elder Award.

Les Wicks (*leswicks.tripod.com/lw.htm*) has been published in over 300 different magazines, anthologies & newspapers in ten languages. His latest collection is *Sea of Heartbeak (Unexpected Resilience)* (2013).

Jennifer Wong (*jenniferwong.co.uk*) received the Hong Kong Young Artist Award in 2014 and is the author of two collections: *Goldfish* (2013) and *Summer Cicadas* (2006).

Nicholas YB Wong is an assistant poetry editor for *Drunken Boat*. His next poetry collection will be published by Kaya Press in 2015. He lives in Hong Kong.

Pui Ying Wong, born in Hong Kong, now resident in Cambridge, MA, is the author of three books of poetry: *Yellow Plum Season* (2010), *Mementos* (2007) and *Sonnet for a New Country* (2008).

Koon Woon (*lockkaukoon.wix.com/chrysanthemum*) and his grandmother lived in Hong Kong when he was a boy before emigrating to the USA. His collection *Water Chasing Water* won a 2014 American Book Award.

CPSIA information can be obtained
at www.ICGtesting.com
Printed in the USA
FFOW04n1351300616
25534FF